Woodland Creatures

Written by Emily Bone
Illustrated by Maribel Lechuga
Designed by Zoe Wray

Woodland consultant: Zoë Simmons
Reading consultant: Alison Kelly

Woods are home to lots
of different animals.

Squirrels run
along branches.

Rabbits live in burrows.
They come out to
find food.

Birds find berries and bugs to eat.

American
robin

Stag
beetle

Wood ants

Tiny mice called dormice
live in tree branches.

They find berries, nuts
and insects to eat.

Hazelnut

Blackberry

A mother dormouse builds a
nest from strips of tree bark.

Her babies are born inside the nest.

Chipmunks live in burrows under the woodland floor.

They come out during the day to look for seeds and nuts to eat.

They push food into their cheeks.

They take the food back to
their burrows.

Birds live high up in woodland trees.

A sapsucker pecks holes in a tree. It licks out the sweet juice inside called sap.

Butterflies feed on the sap too.

Long-tailed tits make nests
in tree branches.

They weave together
moss and cobwebs.

They add feathers to
keep the nest warm.

Lots of bugs live in woods.

Butterflies feed from
woodland flowers.

Swallowtail butterflies

Beetles feed from fallen
trees and leaves.

Hercules
beetle

Spiders build webs
between tree branches.

Orchard
orb weaver
spider

Paper wasps make their nests
from woodland trees.

A queen paper wasp chews
up wood. This makes paper.

She uses the paper
to build a nest.

She lays eggs in the nest.

Queen wasp

Wasp egg

Young wasps hatch out.

Other wasps feed them.

Lots of woodland creatures
are only awake at night.

Bats fly around
catching bugs to eat.

Moth

Tree crickets make a loud chirping noise to find partners.

Chirrup!

Chirrup!

They chirp by rubbing their wings together.

Some owls hunt in woods at night.

A tawny owl spots a vole and swoops down.

It grabs the vole with its sharp claws.

Vole

It takes the vole back to its nest. It feeds the vole to its chicks.

Snakes and lizards live in woods.

They go to sunny areas to warm up in the morning.

Viper

Green lizard

Snakes hunt small animals.
A viper hides in long grass.

A mouse walks past.

The viper rushes up to the
mouse and bites it.

Lots of creatures live around
woodland rivers.

Dragonfly

Kingfishers dive
underwater to
catch food.

Sticklebacks

Otters catch fish and other river creatures.

Trout

They take the fish back to the riverbank and eat them.

21

Beavers make their homes in
woodland rivers.

A beaver bites through a tree.

The tree falls across a river.

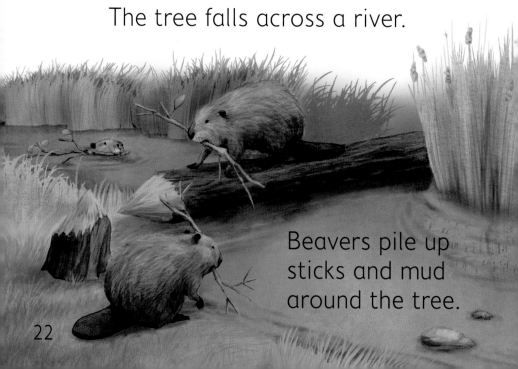

Beavers pile up
sticks and mud
around the tree.

This is called a dam. It stops the river from flowing...

...and makes a big pool.

Beavers build a nest in the pool.

Bears live in some woods.

A mother bear and her cubs live underground during the winter.

They come out in spring to find food. They eat plants and insects.

A male bear spots the cubs.
Sometimes they attack them.

Male bear

The cubs climb a tree
to stay safe.

Deer live in groups called herds.

They eat leaves, grass and young trees.

Male deer have antlers. They use their antlers to fight other deer.

Deer have babies called fawns.

A mother deer gives birth to a fawn.
She licks it clean.

The fawn drinks milk from her mother.

Sometimes woodland trees die.
They're home to many creatures.

Bats rest inside dead trees.

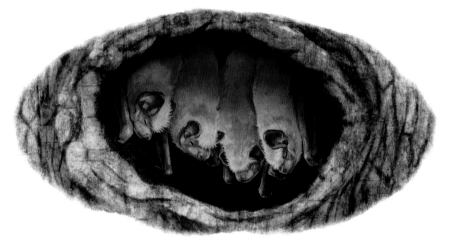

Woodpeckers make nests
inside them.

Some trees fall down when they die.
Animals live in the trees.

Fox and cubs

Bugs live on the wood.

Snail

Millipede

Beetle

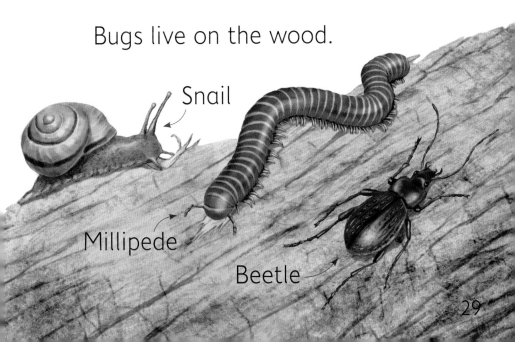

Woods can get very cold in winter.
There's not much food.

Squirrels bury nuts in the summer.
They dig them up to eat during winter.

Rattlesnakes hide away through the
winter. They don't eat anything.

30

Some trees still have berries
that grew in the summer.
Birds flock to eat them.

Waxwings

Rowan berries

It warms up again in the spring.
There is lots of food for woodland
creatures to eat.

Waxwings
feed berries
to their chicks.

Digital retouching by John Russell

First published in 2017 by Usborne Publishing Ltd., Usborne House, 83-85 Saffron Hill, London EC1N 8RT England. www.usborne.com Copyright © 2017 Usborne Publishing Ltd. The name Usborne and the devices ♀⊕ are Trade Marks of Usborne Publishing Ltd. All rights reserved. No part of this publication may be reproduced, stored in a retrieval system, or transmitted in any form or by any means, electronic, mechanical, photocopying, recording or otherwise without the prior permission of the publisher. First published in America 2017. UE.